Little

A Royal Shakespeare Company Production

Roald Dahl's

Matilda

THE MUSICAL

MUSIC & LYRICS BY TIM MINCHIN

First performance at The Courtyard Theatre,
Stratford-upon-Avon, 9 November 2010

First performance at The Cambridge Theatre,
London, 25 October 2011

First performance at The Shubert Theatre,
New York, 4 March 2013

With thanks to Tim Minchin, Chris Nightingale,
Caroline Chignell and Kevin Wright.

NOVELLO PUBLISHING LIMITED
part of The Music Sales Group
London/New York/Paris/Sydney/Copenhagen/Berlin/Madrid/Hong Kong/Tokyo

Published by
Novello Publishing Limited
14-15 Berners Street, London, W1T 3LJ, UK.

Exclusive distributors:
Music Sales Limited
Distribution Centre, Newmarket Road,
Bury St Edmunds, Suffolk, IP33 3YB, UK.

Music Sales Pty Limited
4th floor, Lisgar House, 30-32 Carrington Street,
Sydney, NSW 2000, Australia.

Edited by Ruth Power.
Music arranged by Simon Foxley.
Music processed by Paul Ewers Music Design.
Photographs courtesy of the original London cast at
The Cambridge Theatre by Manuel Harlan. © Royal Shakespeare Company.
Cover image artwork and design by aka.

Printed in the EU.

www.musicsales.com

Your Guarantee of Quality:
As publishers, we strive to produce every book
to the highest commercial standards.

The book has been carefully designed to minimise awkward
page turns and to make playing from it a real pleasure.
Particular care has been given to specifying
acid-free, neutral-sized paper made from pulps
which have not been elemental chlorine bleached.

This pulp is from farmed sustainable forests
and was produced with special regard for the environment.

Throughout, the printing and binding have
been planned to ensure a sturdy, attractive
publication which should give years of enjoyment.

If your copy fails to meet our high standards,
please inform us and we will gladly replace it.

Naughty

Words & Music by Tim Minchin

They nev - er stood a chance.

-ev - i - ta - ble.

They were writ - ten that way.

Cm(add9)/E♭

In - no - cent vic - tims of their sto - ry. Like

In - no - cent vic - tims of their sto - ry. Like

G   D   C

Ro - me - o and Ju - li - et, 'twas writ-ten in the stars be - fore they e - ven met

Ro - me - o and Ju - li - et, 'twas writ-ten in the stars be - fore they e - ven met

that love and fate and a touch of stu - pid - i - ty would

that love and fate and a touch of stu - pid - i - ty would

rob them of their hope of liv - ing hap - pi - ly. The end - ings are of - ten a

rob them of their hope of liv - ing hap - pi - ly. The end - ings are of - ten a

Cm(add9)/E♭   G

lit - tle bit gor - y.   I won - der why they did - n't just
(Finger snaps)

lit - tle bit gor - y.   I won - der why they did - n't just
(Finger snaps)

D   C   G

change their sto - ry. We're told we have to do what we're told but sure-

change their sto - ry. We're told we have to do what we're told but sure-

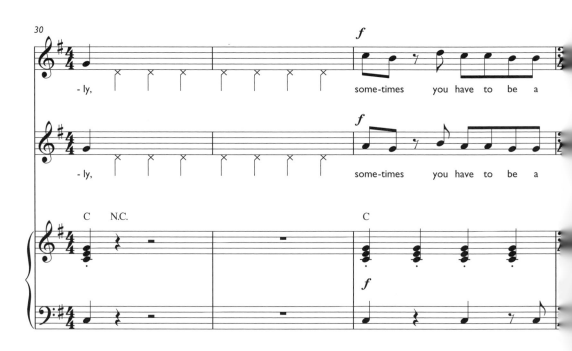

- ly, some-times you have to be a

- ly, some-times you have to be a

lit - tle bit naugh - ty.   Just be - cause you find that life's

lit - tle bit naugh - ty.   Just   be -

___ not fair,___ it___ does-n't mean that you just have to grin and bear___ it.___

- cause   life's   not   fair,   you   don't   have   to

don't let it stop you. Don't let them

must-n't let a lit-tle thing like lit - tle stop__ you.__ If you sit a - round and let them

G/B   Am

get on top,__ you might as well be say - ing you think that it's o - kay, and

get on top,__ you might as well be say - ing you think that it's o - kay, and

D⁶   B⁷/D♯   N.C.

11

that's not right!   And if it's not___ right,

that's not right!   And if it's not___ right,

B   B/D#   Em   D   Cmaj7   C   D/F#   G

you have to put it___ right.   But

you have to put it___ right.   But

Em   F#7   B7

no - bod - y else___ is gon - na put it right for me, no - bod - y but me is gon - na

no - bod - y else___ is gon - na put it right for me, no - bod - y but me is gon - na

change my sto - ry; some - times you have to be a lit - tle bit naugh - ty.

change my sto - ry; some - times you have to be a lit - tle bit naugh - ty.

13

School Song

Words & Music by Tim Minchin

-dy. And e-ven if you put in heaps of ef-fort, you're just wast-ing en-er-

-dy. And e-ven if you put in heaps of ef-fort, you're just wast-ing en-er-

-gy, 'cause your life as you know it is an-cient his-to-ry.

-gy, 'cause your life as you know it is an-cient his-to-ry.

I have suf-fered in this jail.__ Have been trapped in-side this cage for a-ges, this liv-ing

I have suf-fered in this jail.__ Have been trapped in-side this cage for a-ges, this liv-ing

'ell. But if I try I can re - mem - ber, back be-fore my life had

'ell. But if I try I can re - mem - ber, back be-fore my life had

end - ed, be - fore my hap - py days were o - ver, be - fore I first heard the

end - ed, be - fore my hap - py days were o - ver, be - fore I first heard the

peal - ing of the bell. Like you, I was cu - ri - ous, so in - no - cent I

peal - ing of the bell. Like you, I was cu - ri - ous, so in - no - cent I

21

asked a thou - sand ques - tions. But, un - less you want to suf - fer, lis - ten up and I will

asked a thou - sand ques - tions. But, un - less you want to suf - fer, lis - ten up and I will

F

A⁷⁽♭⁹⁾

23

teach you a thing or two. You lis - ten here, my dear, you'll be pun - ished so se -

teach you a thing or two. You lis - ten here, my dear, you'll be pun - ished so se -

A

Gm

ƒ

mf

mf

18

-vere-ly if you step out of line. And if you cry it will be dou-ble. You should stay out of trou-ble and re-mem-ber to be

-vere-ly if you step out of line. And if you cry it will be dou-ble. You should stay out of trou-ble and re-mem-ber to be

ex-treme-ly care-ful.   And so you think you're

ex-treme-ly care-ful.   And so you think you're

A, B, C, D, E, F, G, H, I, J, K, L, M, N, O, P, Q, R, S, T, U, V, W,— X.

A, B, C, D, E, F, G, H, I, J, K, L, M, N, O, P, Q, R, S, T, U, V, W,— X.

Why, why, why, why, why, why, why?___ Why? Just you wait for Phys-Ed!

Why, why, why, why, why, why, why?___ Why? Just you wait for Phys-Ed!

When I Grow Up

Words & Music by Tim Minchin

22

23

that you have to fight____ be - neath___ the bed each night to

that you have to fight____ be - neath___ the bed each night to

Am⁷(♭5)   G

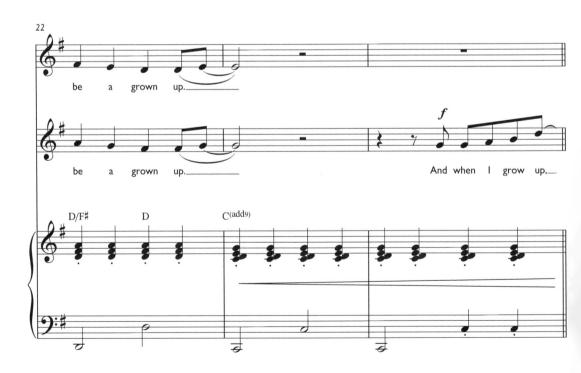

be a grown up._____

be a grown up._____ And when I grow up,___

D/F♯   D   C(add9)

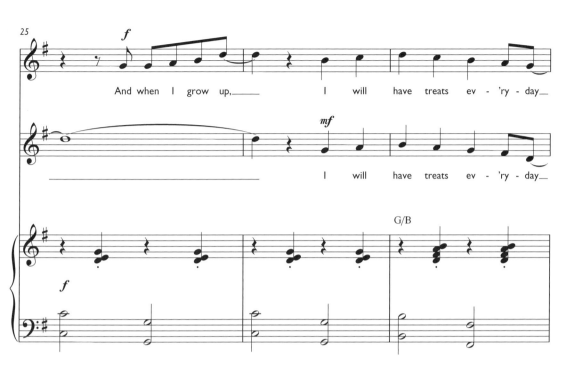

And when I grow up,_____ I will have treats ev - 'ry - day__

I will have treats ev - 'ry - day__

G/B

__ and I'll play_____ with things__ that mum_____ pre - tends that mums__

__ and I'll play_____ with things__ that mum_____ pre - tends that mums__

Am⁷

25

26

day just ly - ing in_____ the sun,_____ and I won't burn 'cause I'll_____

day just ly - ing in_____ the sun,_____ and I won't burn 'cause I'll_____

_____ be all_____ grown up,_____ when I_____ grow

_____ be all_____ grown up,_____ when I_____ grow

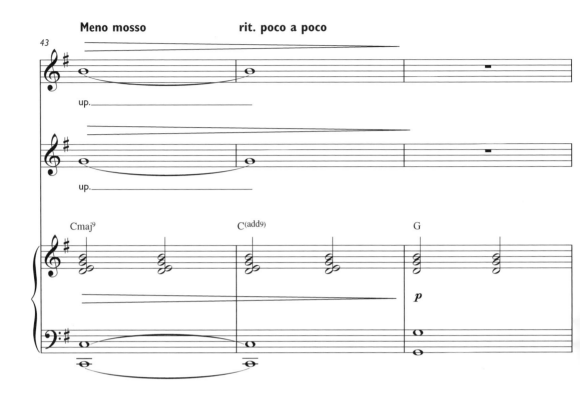

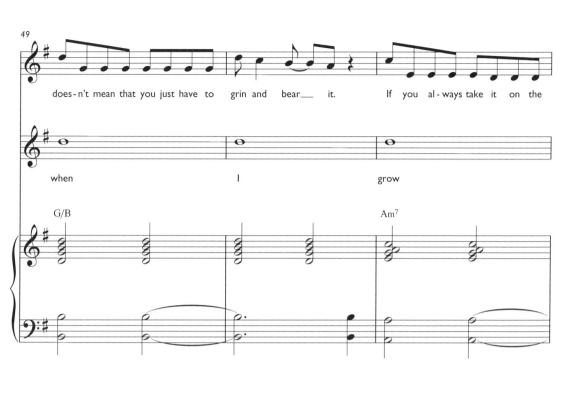

does-n't mean that you just have to grin and bear___ it.   If you al-ways take it on the

when   I   grow

chin and   wear it   noth-ing   will change.   When I   grow

up,   noth-ing   will change.

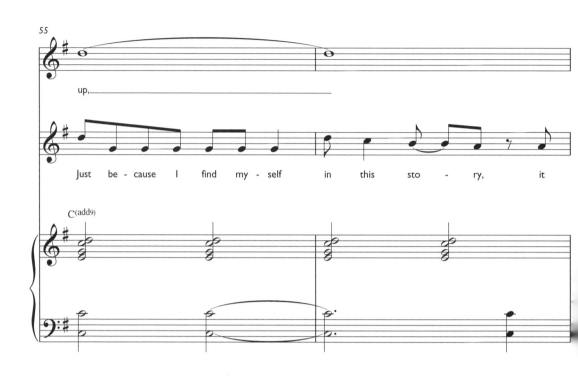

55

up,_____

Just be - cause I find my - self in this sto - ry, it

C(add9)

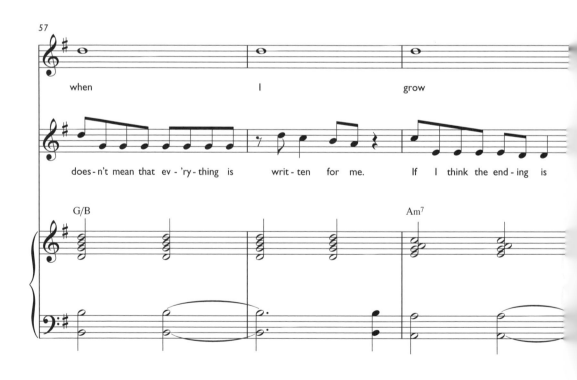

57

when I grow

does - n't mean that ev - 'ry - thing is writ - ten for me. If I think the end - ing is

G/B

Am⁷

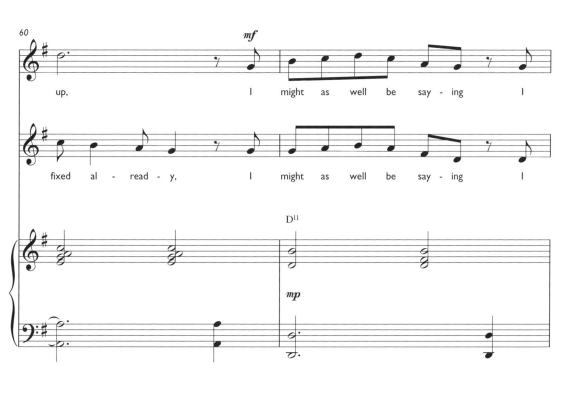

up, | I might as well be say - ing | I

fixed al - read - y, | I might as well be say - ing | I

think that it's O. K. | And that's not right!

think that it's O. K. | And that's not right!

My House

Words & Music by Tim Minchin

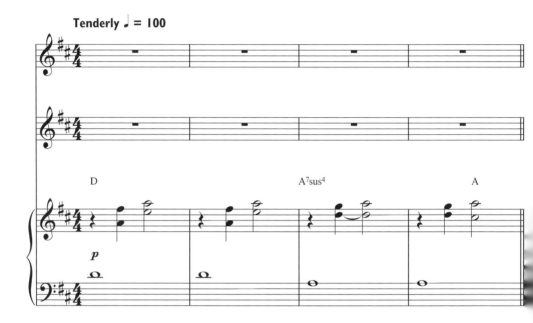

On these walls, I hang won-der-ful pic-tures.

Through this win-dow I can

By this lamp I can read, and
watch the sea - sons change. and

G   D/F♯

I, I am_ set free! And when it's cold out -
I, I am_ set free! And when it's cold out -

Em   A   D

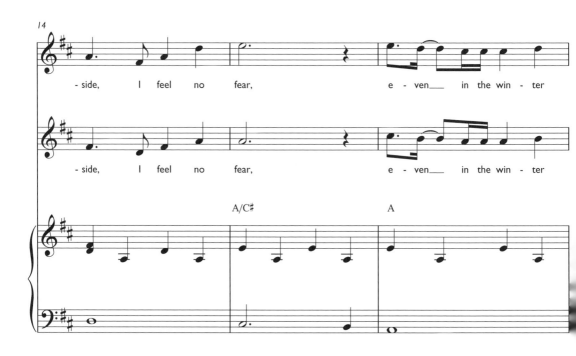

and there is no-where I would___ rath - er

and there is no-where I would___ rath - er

D/F♯   G   D/F♯

be.   *mp* It is - n't much, but

be.   *p* It is - n't much, but

A   G   D/F♯

p

it is___ e - nough for me.

it is___ e - nough for me.

Em⁷ D

It is-n't much, but it is___ e - nough for me.

It is-n't much, but it is___ e - nough for me.

Em D/F♯ G A¹¹ D

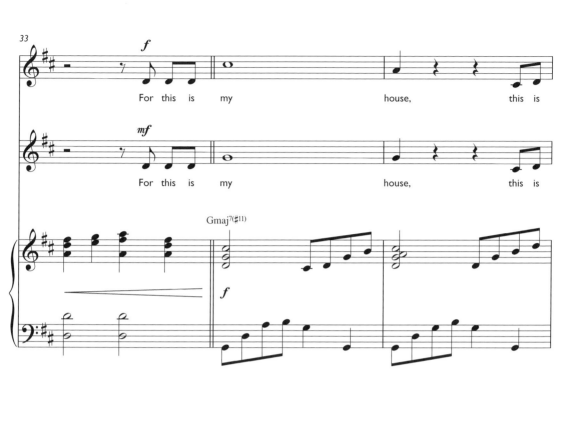

For this is my house, this is

For this is my house, this is

my_____ house. It is - n't much, but

my_____ house. It is - n't much, but

it is___ e - nough for me. This is my___

it is___ e - nough for me. This is my___

G   A^{7}sus^4 D   Em^7 D/F$\sharp$ D Gmaj$^{7(\sharp11)}$

house,   this is my___ house.

house,   this is my___ house.

Gmaj^7 F$\sharp$m^7

It is - n't much, but it is___ e-nough for me.

It is - n't much, but it is___ e-nough for me.

Em⁷   D/F#   G   A¹¹   D

rit. poco a poco

It is - n't much, but it is___ e - nough_____ for me.

It is - n't much, but it is___ e - nough_____ for me.

Em⁷   D/F#   G   A⁵   N.C.

Revolting Children

Words & Music by Tim Minchin

re - volt - ing songs us - ing_____ re - volt - ing rhymes. We'll be_____

re - volt - ing songs us - ing_____ re - volt - ing rhymes. We'll be_____

re - volt - ing child - ren till our re - volt - ing's done and we'll

re - volt - ing child - ren till our re - volt - ing's done and we'll

have the Trunch - bull bolt - ing, we're re - volt - ing! We are___

have the Trunch - bull bolt - ing, we're re - volt - ing! We are___

- volt - ing! We can S - P - L how we

- volt - ing! We can S - P - L how we

like! If e- nough of us are wrong, wrong is right! Ev -'ry - one! N - O - R - T -

like! If e- nough of us are wrong, wrong is right! Ev -'ry - one! N - O - R - T -

- WHY? 'Cause we're a lit - tle bit naugh - ty! You say we ough-ta stay in - side the

- WHY? 'Cause we're a lit - tle bit naugh - ty! You say we ough-ta stay in - side the

line. But if we dis-o-bey at the same time, there is noth-ing that the Trunch-bull can

line. But if we dis-o-bey at the same time, there is noth-ing that the Trunch-bull can

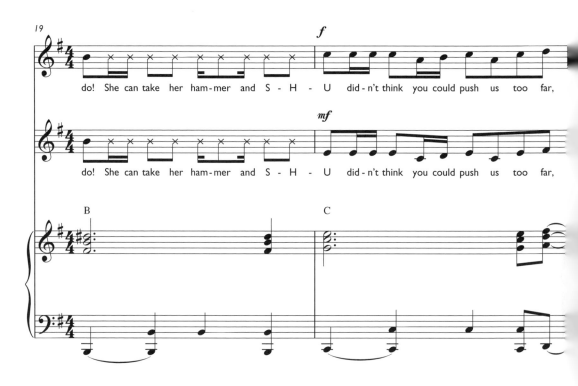

do! She can take her ham-mer and S - H - U did-n't think you could push us too far,

do! She can take her ham-mer and S - H - U did-n't think you could push us too far,

but there's no go-ing back now, we R-E-V-O-L-T-I-N. We'll S-

but there's no go-ing back now, we R-E-V-O-L-T-I-N. We'll S-

-I-N-G,___ U-S - I-N-G.___ We'll be___ R-E-V-O-L-T-

-I-N-G,___ U-S - I-N-G.___ We'll be___ R-E-V-O-L-T-

- I - N - G.___ It is 2 - L - 8 - 4 - U E - R - E - volt - ing! We are___

- I - N - G.___ It is 2 - L - 8 - 4 - U E - R - E - volt - ing! We are___

___ re-volt-ing child-ren liv-ing in___ re-volt-ing times. We sing___ re-volt-ing songs us-ing___

___ re-volt-ing child-ren liv-ing in___ re-volt-ing times. We sing___ re-volt-ing songs us-ing___

re-volt-ing rhymes. We'll be___ re-volt-ing child-ren till our re-volt-ing's done. It is

re-volt-ing rhymes. We'll be___ re-volt-ing child-ren till our re-volt-ing's done. It is

2 - L - 8 - 4 - U! We are_ 2 - L - 8 - 4 - U E - R - E - volt-ing!

2 - L - 8 - 4 - U! We are_ 2 - L - 8 - 4 - U E - R - E - volt-ing!